by Jerry Pallotta
Illustrated by Ralph Masiello
Title by Neil Pallotta

# THE ICKY BUG ALPHABET BOOK

Charlesbridge

For Julia, Joey III, Jimmy, Lauren, Jenna, A.J., Lisa, Bobby, Johnny, Alison, David, Jr., Lady Diane, Christine, Elizabeth, Emily, Meaghan, Daniel, Jr., Sheila, Neil, Eric, Jill, Brittany, Meghan and . . .

Published by
Charlesbridge Publishing
85 Main Street
Watertown, MA 02172-4411
(617) 926-0329

**Library of Congress Cataloging-in-Publication Data**
Pallotta, Jerry.
   The icky bug alphabet book / by Jerry Pallotta; Ralph Masiello, illustrator.
       p.    cm.
   Summary:   Introduces the characteristics and activities of insects and other crawly creatures from A to Z, beginning with the ant and concluding with the zebra butterfly.
   ISBN 0-88106-676-1 (library reinforced)
   ISBN 0-88106-456-4 (trade hardcover)
   ISBN 0-88106-450-5 (softcover)
   1. Insects–Juvenile literature.   2. English language–Alphabet–Juvenile literature.
[1. Insects. 2. Alphabet.]   I. Masiello, Ralph, ill.   II. Title.
QL467.2.P32   1986b
595.7 — dc20                                                      89-60421
[E]                                                                        CIP
                                                                              AC

Printed in the United States of America
(sc) 20  19  18  17  16  15  14  13
(hc) 10   9   8   7   6   5   4   3

Printed on Recycled Paper.

Books by Jerry Pallotta
   *The Icky Bug Alphabet Book*
   *The Icky Bug Counting Book*
   *The Bird Alphabet Book*
   *The Ocean Alphabet Book*
   *The Flower Alphabet Book*
   *The Yucky Reptile Alphabet Book*
   *The Frog Alphabet Book*
   *The Furry Alphabet Book*
   *The Dinosaur Alphabet Book*
   *The Underwater Alphabet Book*
   *The Victory Garden Vegetable Alphabet Book*
   *The Extinct Alphabet Book*
   *The Desert Alphabet Book*
   *The Spice Alphabet Book*
   *The Make Your Own Alphabet Book*
   *Going Lobstering*
   *Cuenta los insectos (The Icky Bug Counting Book*

Special thanks to Donald Salvatore of the Museum of Science, Boston, Massachusetts.

# A a

**A** is for Alphabet Book.
**A** is also for Ant. Ants are hard
workers. Ants are able to carry
things that are larger and heavier
than they are. They always seem
to be trying to build something.

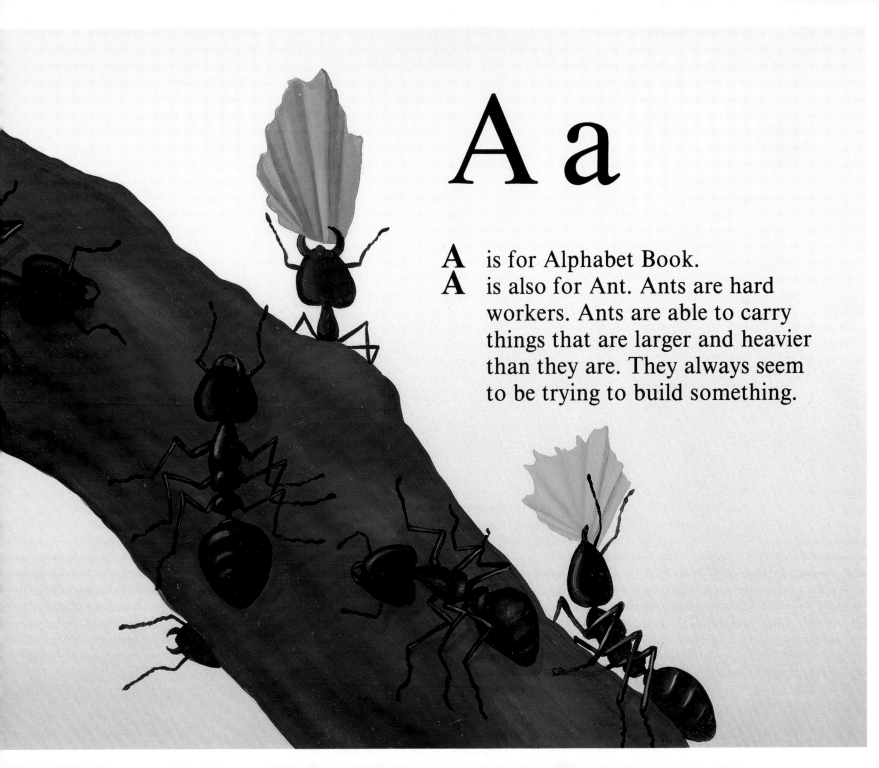

# B b

**B** is for Bumblebee. Because the Bumblebee is furry, it is able to stay outside in cooler weather than other types of bees. Bumblebees fly from flower to flower collecting nectar to make honey.

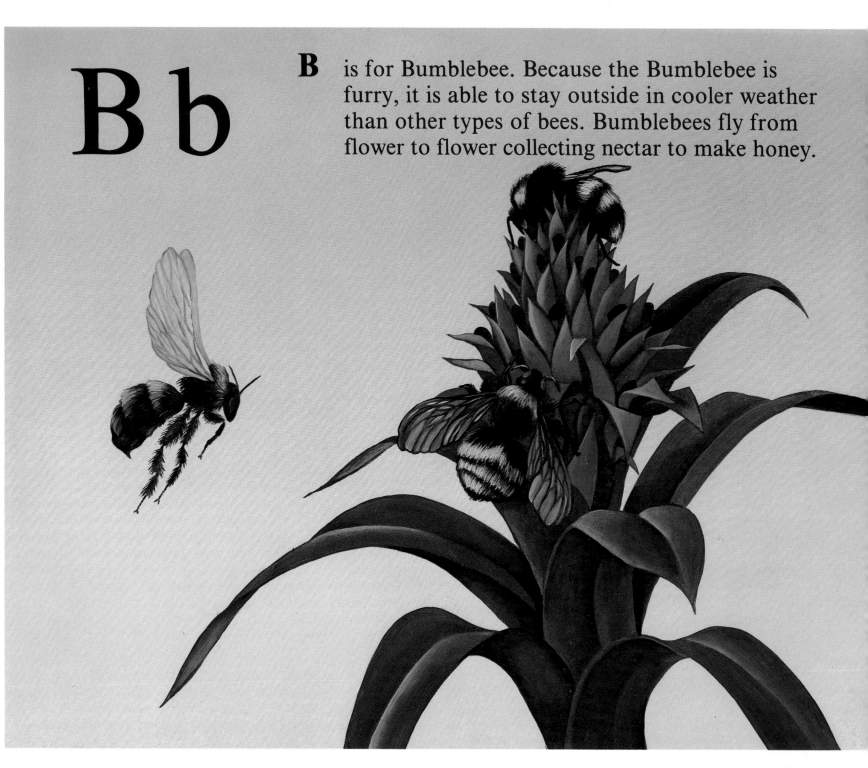

# Cc

C is for Cricket. The Cricket likes to hide under things. It makes noise by rubbing its wings together. Isn't it fun to listen to lots of Crickets at night?

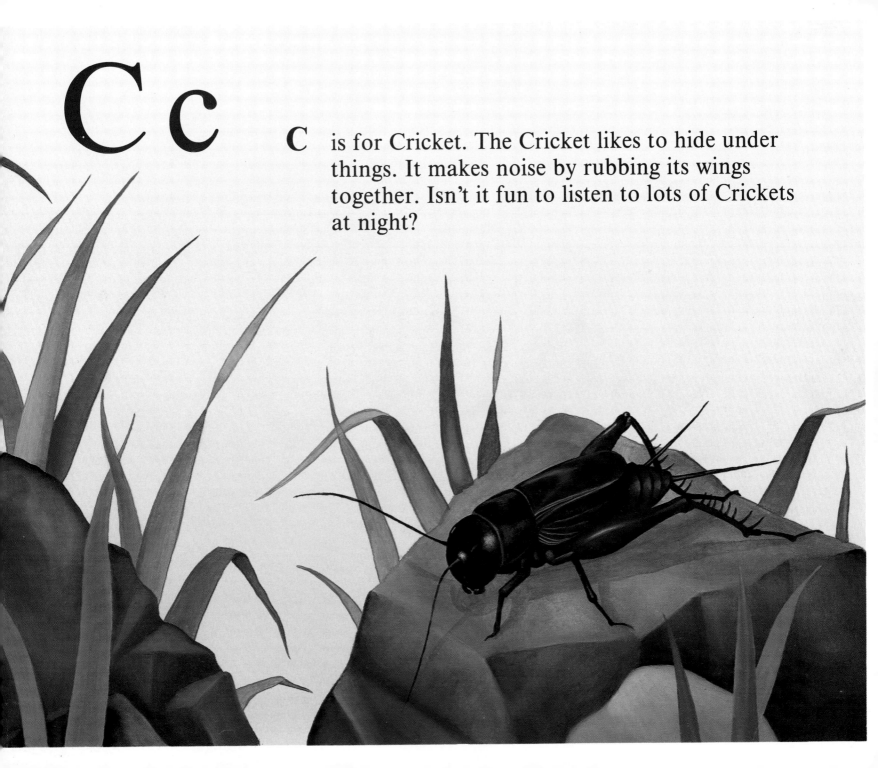

# D d

**D** is for Dragonfly. The Dragonfly has four wings. When Dragonflies stop flying and take a rest, they are unable to fold their wings back.

**E** is for Earwig. No one seems to know how the Earwig got its name. It does not crawl into people's ears. It has a pincher at the tail end of its body.

E e

# F f

**F** is for Firefly. Fireflies shine like lightbulbs in the dark. When they light up, they can find each other more easily. Fireflies are easy to catch because they fly so slowly.

**G** is for Grasshopper. Grasshoppers can jump really well. If you try to catch one, it will usually jump away just as you are about to touch it.

G g

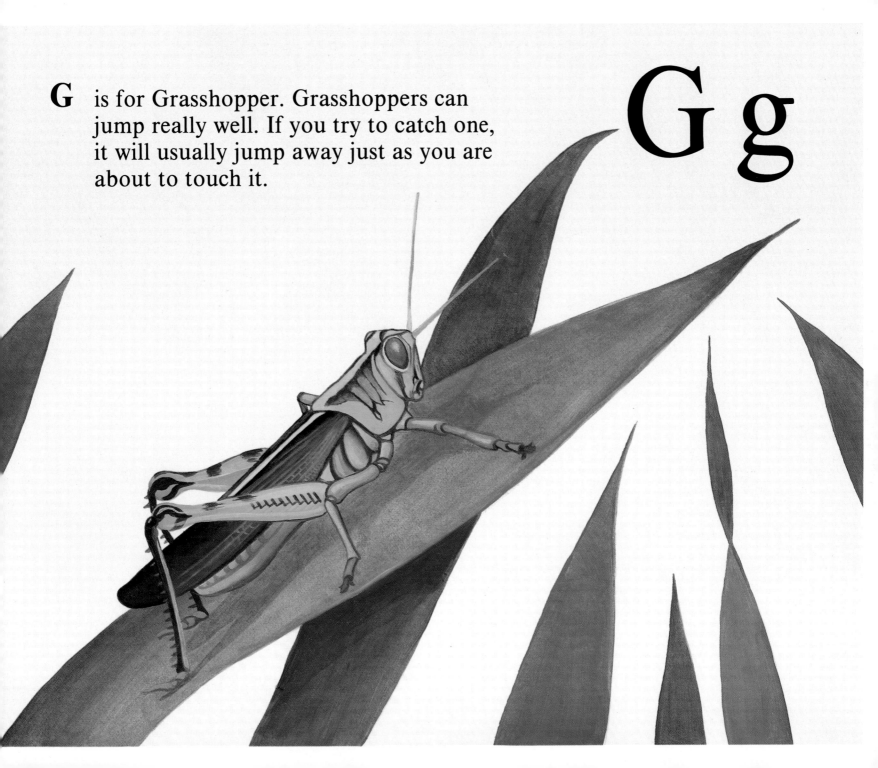

# H h

**H** is for Horsefly. The greenheaded Horsefly has pretty eyes, but it has a terrible bite. If one of them lands on you, be careful! Yikes! Push it away!

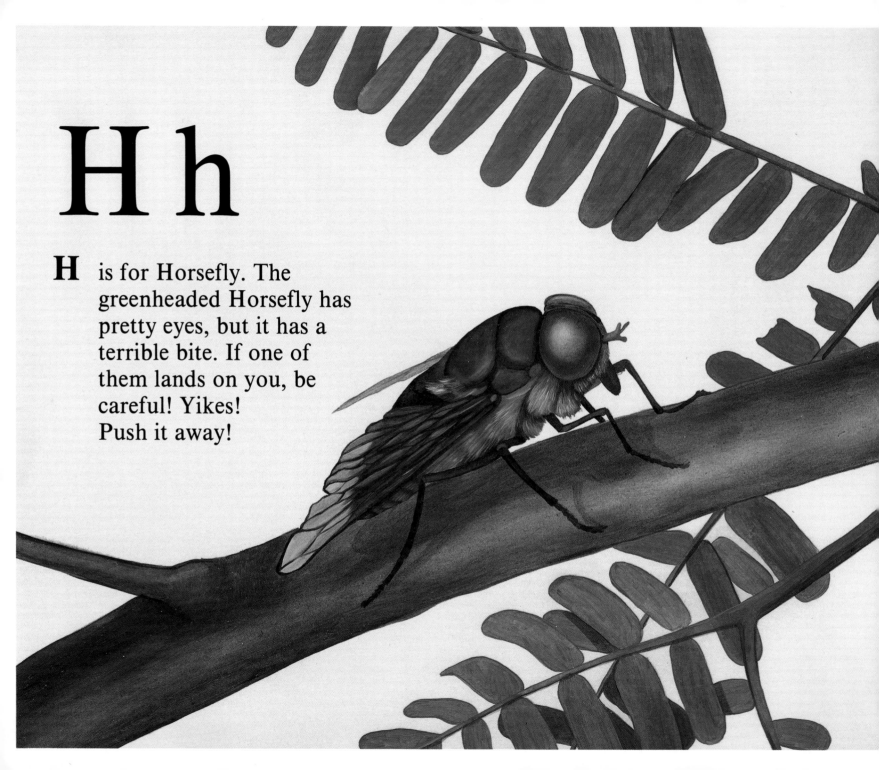

**I** is for Io Moth. The Io Moth has two spots on its lower wings that look like eyes. When birds go near these moths and see the spots, they become startled and fly away.

Ii

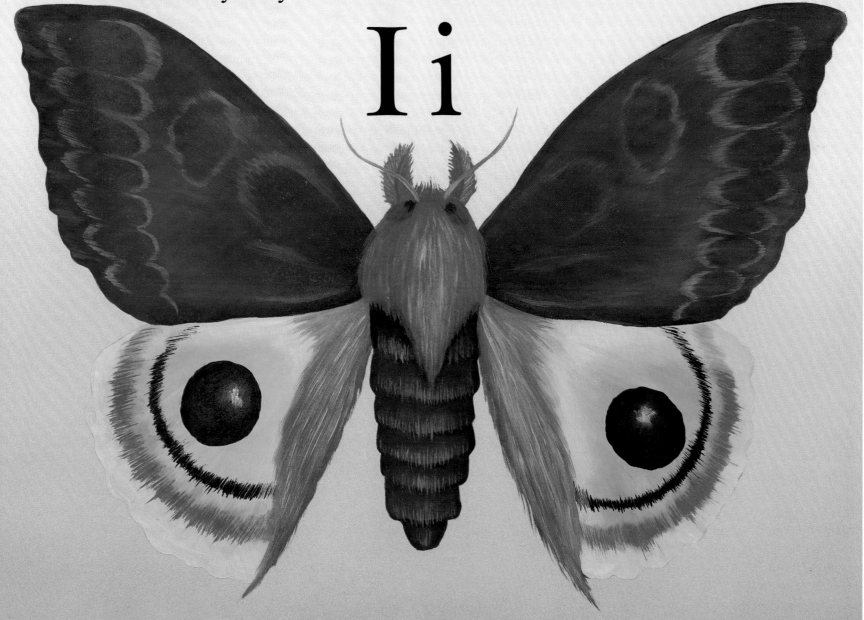

# J j

**J** is for Japanese Beetle. These beetles love to eat flowers. Sometimes they eat so much that they cause lots of damage to plants.

# K k

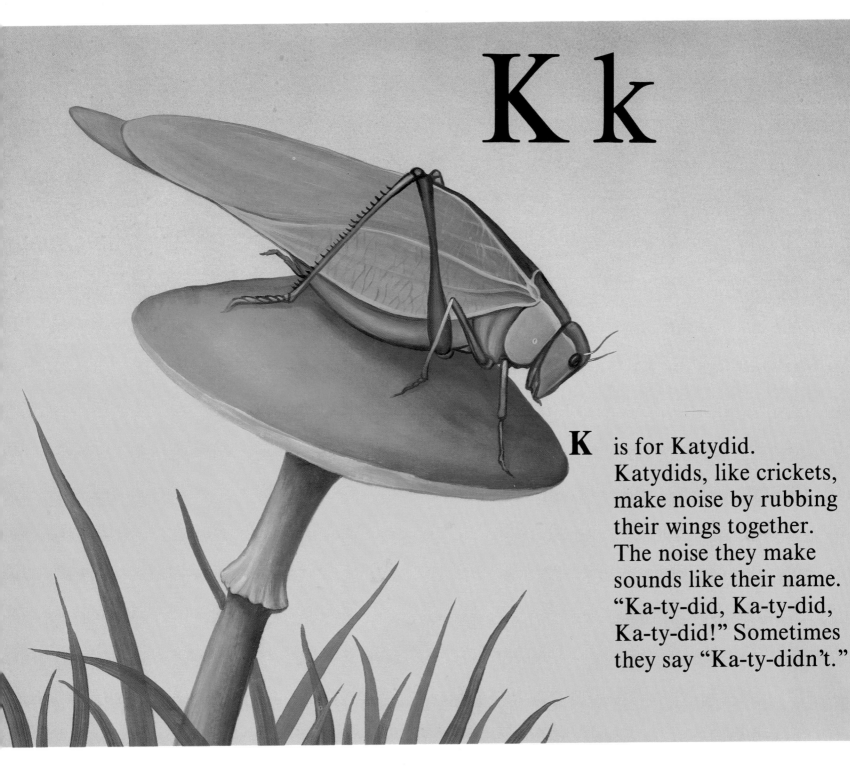

**K** is for Katydid. Katydids, like crickets, make noise by rubbing their wings together. The noise they make sounds like their name. "Ka-ty-did, Ka-ty-did, Ka-ty-did!" Sometimes they say "Ka-ty-didn't."

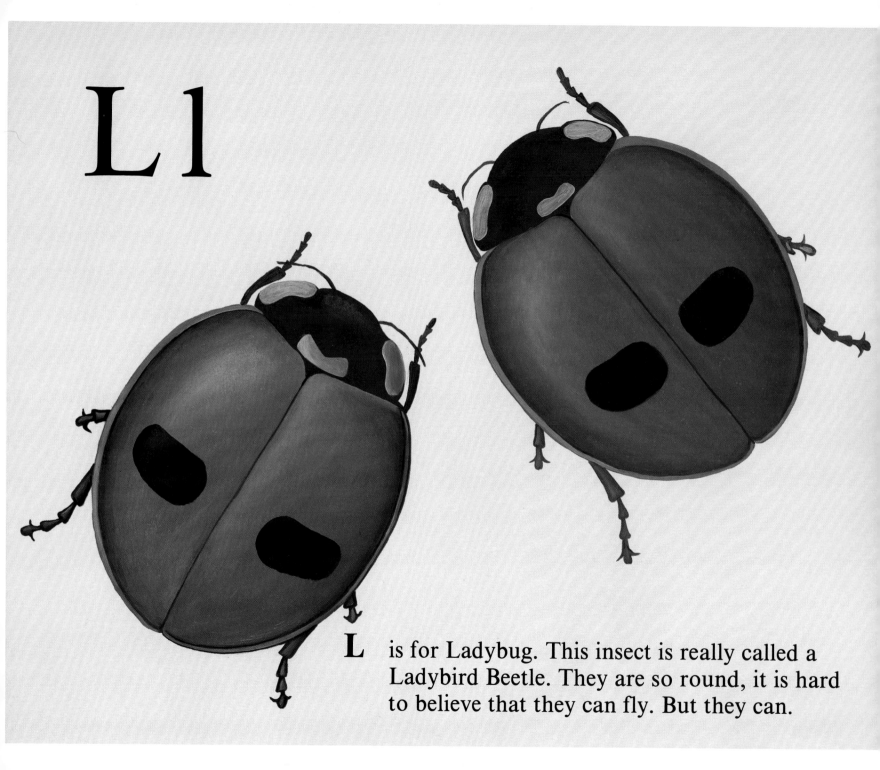

# L l

**L** is for Ladybug. This insect is really called a Ladybird Beetle. They are so round, it is hard to believe that they can fly. But they can.

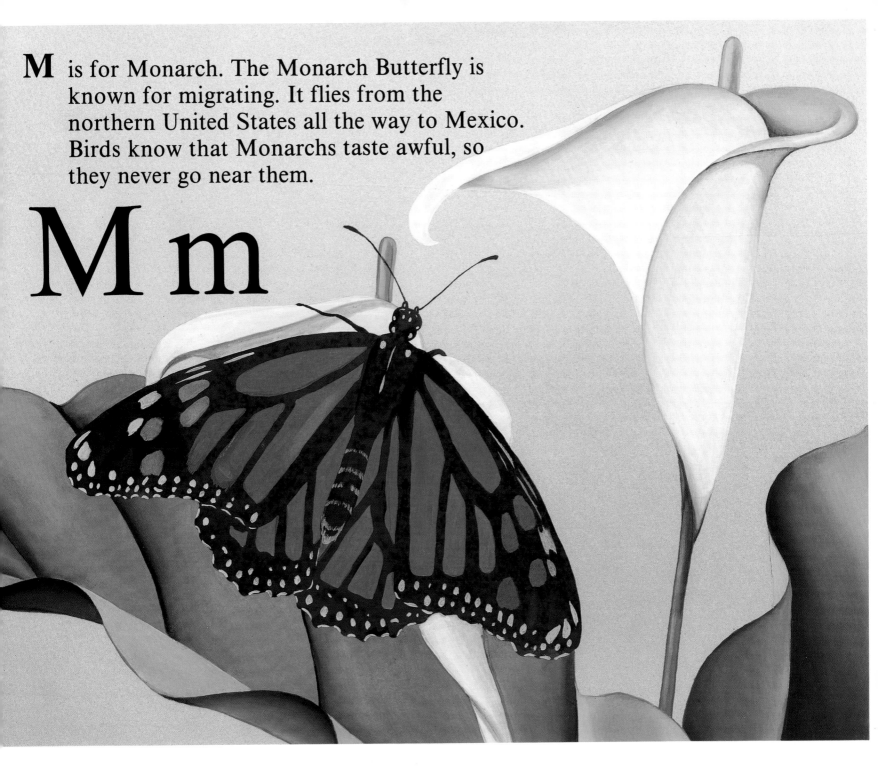

**M** is for Monarch. The Monarch Butterfly is
known for migrating. It flies from the
northern United States all the way to Mexico.
Birds know that Monarchs taste awful, so
they never go near them.

# M m

# N n

**N** is for No-see-ums. No-see-ums is a word for tiny insects that are almost impossible to see. They are flies that are really called midges. They can make people miserable because they bite.

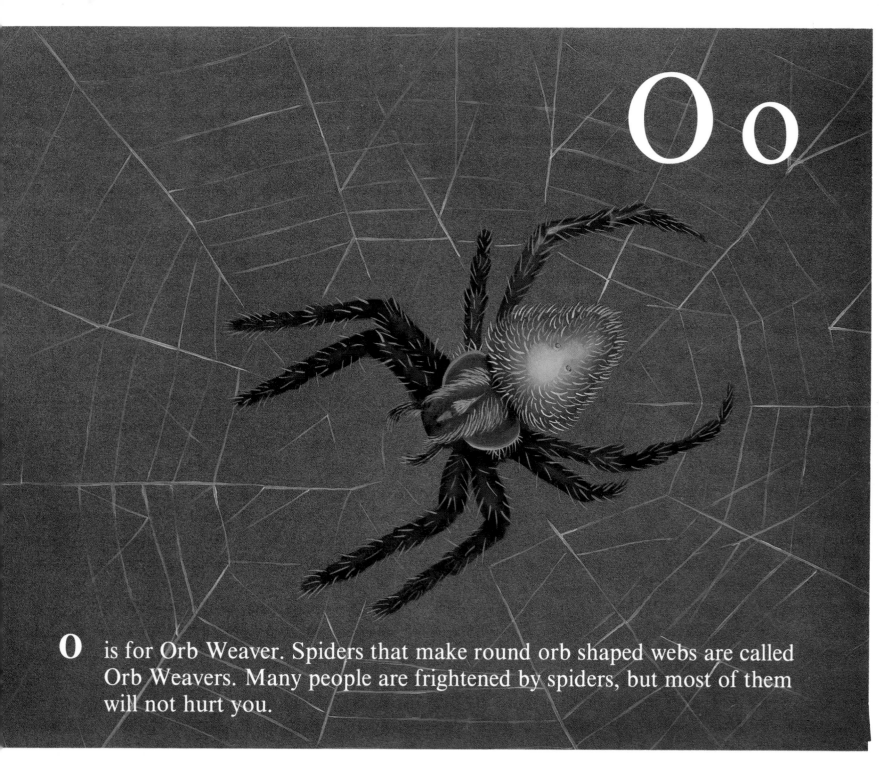

**O o**

**O** is for Orb Weaver. Spiders that make round orb shaped webs are called Orb Weavers. Many people are frightened by spiders, but most of them will not hurt you.

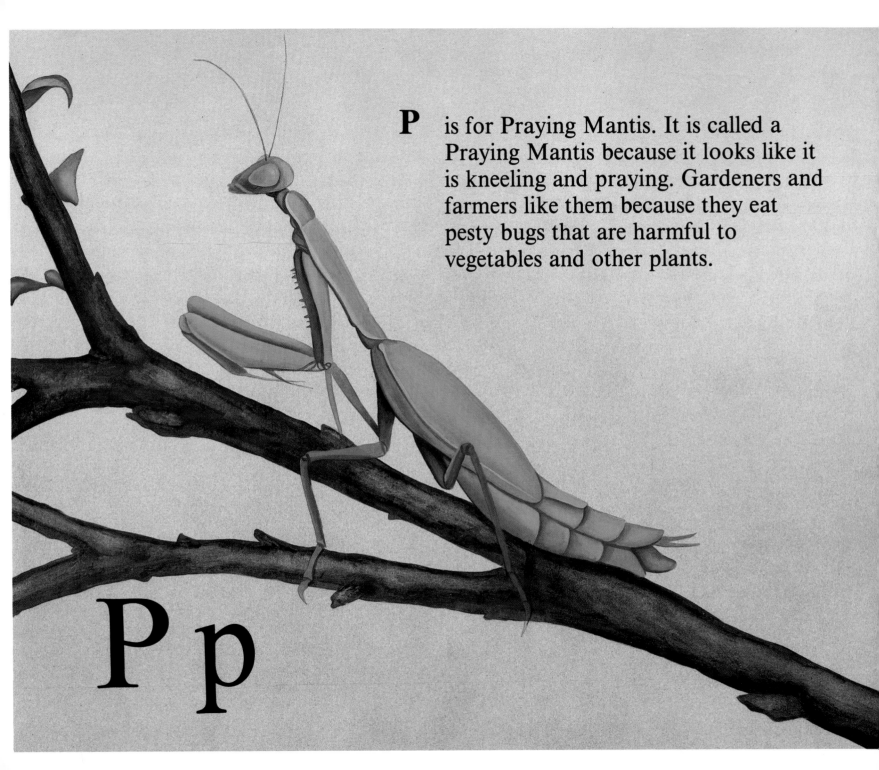

**P** is for Praying Mantis. It is called a Praying Mantis because it looks like it is kneeling and praying. Gardeners and farmers like them because they eat pesty bugs that are harmful to vegetables and other plants.

P p

**Q** is for Queen Bee. In a bee hive there is only one Queen Bee. She can lay thousands of eggs per day. All of the other bees in the hive take good care of the Queen Bee.

Q q

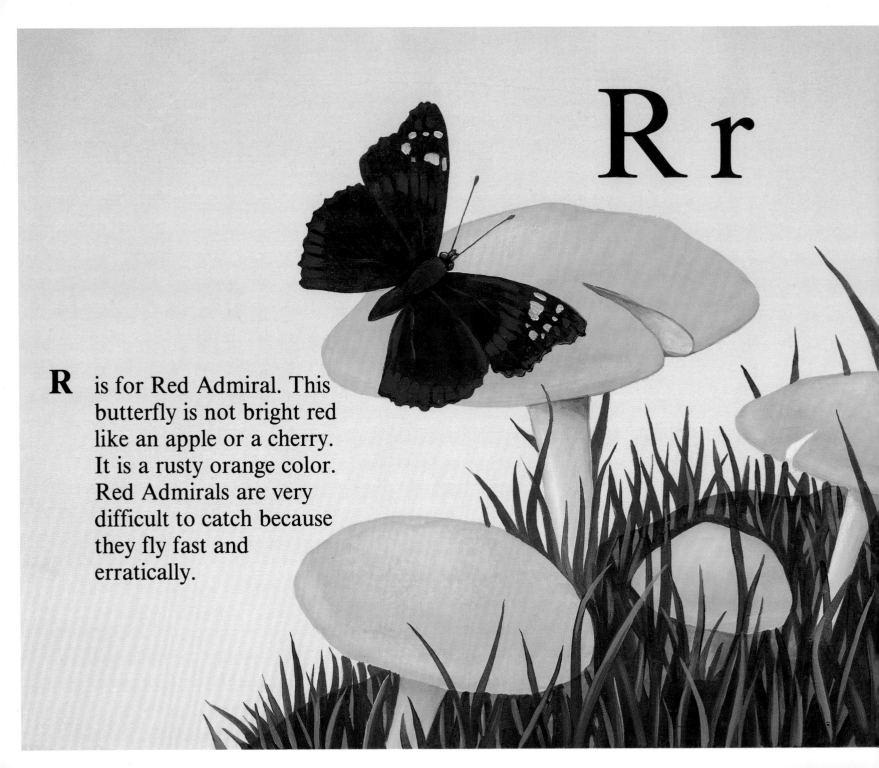

# R r

**R** is for Red Admiral. This butterfly is not bright red like an apple or a cherry. It is a rusty orange color. Red Admirals are very difficult to catch because they fly fast and erratically.

# S s

**s** is for Scorpion. Scorpions are really scary looking. They have two front pinchers just like lobsters. At the end of their tails, they have stingers. Would you like to be stung by a Scorpion?

# T t

**T** is for Tarantula. The Tarantula is a big furry spider. It can grow to be as large as your hand. Tarantulas and Scorpions are found in warm climates.

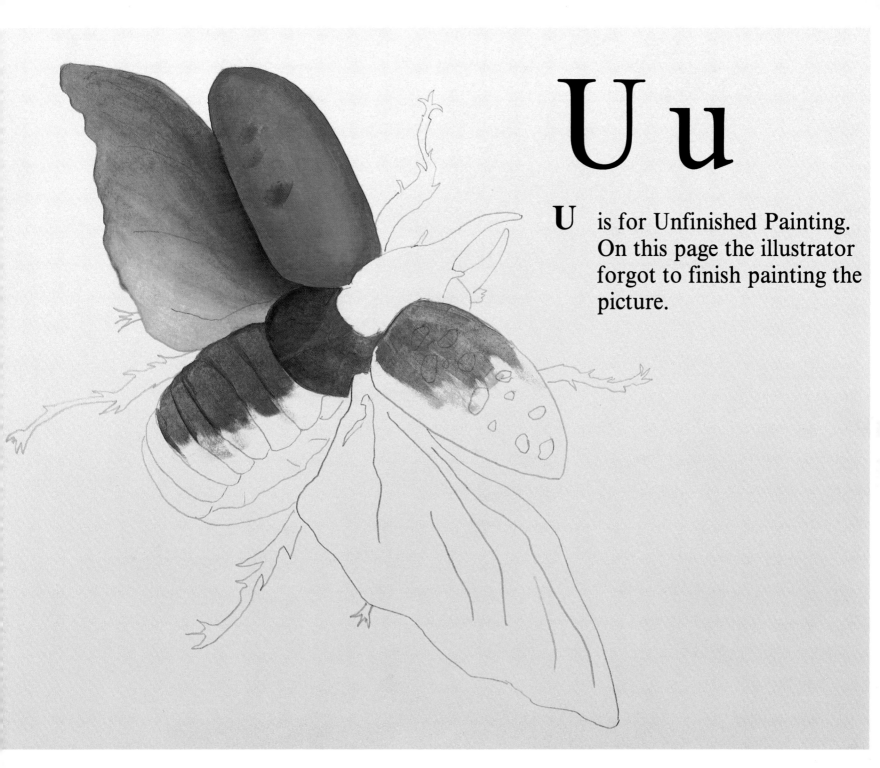

# U u

**U** is for Unfinished Painting. On this page the illustrator forgot to finish painting the picture.

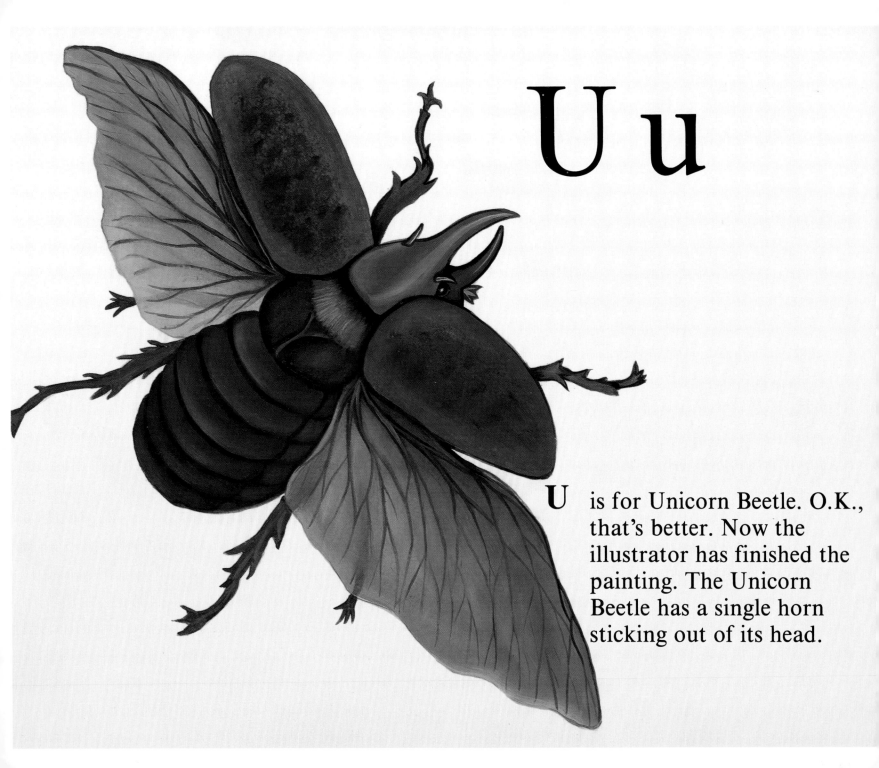

# U u

U is for Unicorn Beetle. O.K.,
that's better. Now the
illustrator has finished the
painting. The Unicorn
Beetle has a single horn
sticking out of its head.

# V v

V is for Velvet Mite. These creatures are red and so small that you can hardly see them. About thirty of them could fit on the fingernail of your thumb.

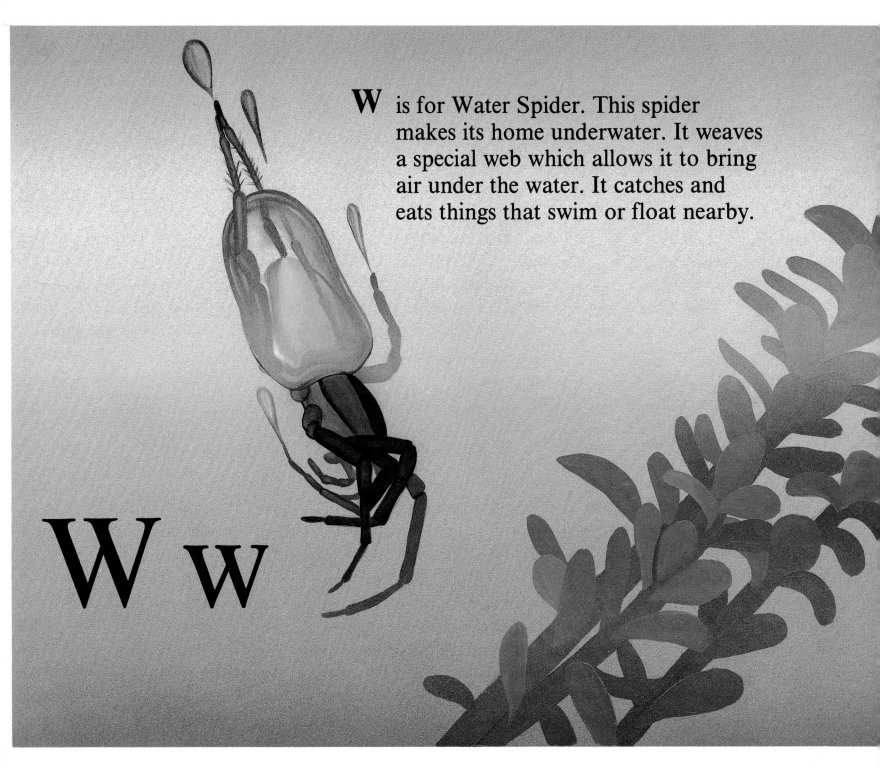

**W** is for Water Spider. This spider makes its home underwater. It weaves a special web which allows it to bring air under the water. It catches and eats things that swim or float nearby.

W w

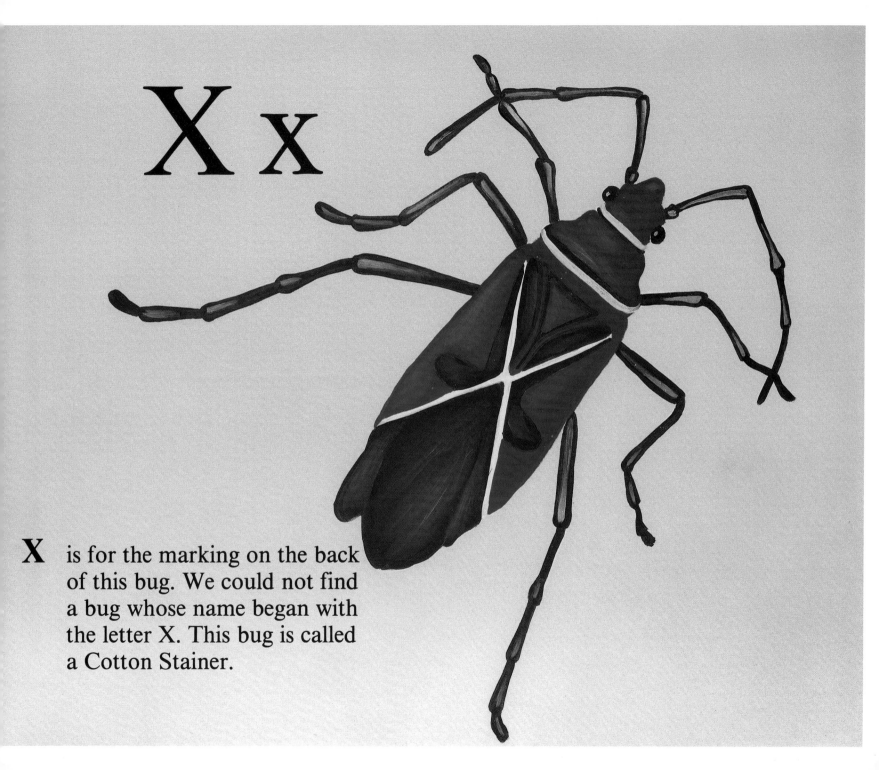

# X x

**X** is for the marking on the back of this bug. We could not find a bug whose name began with the letter X. This bug is called a Cotton Stainer.

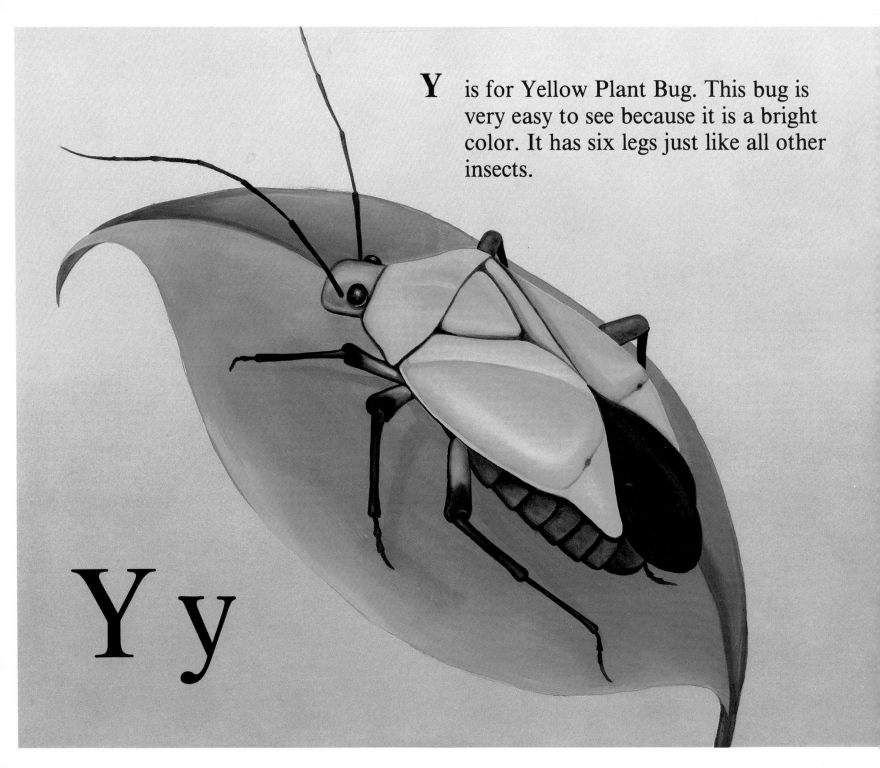

**Y** is for Yellow Plant Bug. This bug is very easy to see because it is a bright color. It has six legs just like all other insects.

Y y

# Z z

**Z** is for Zillions of Zebra Butterflies. Zillions of them flying all at once would be a beautiful sight to see.

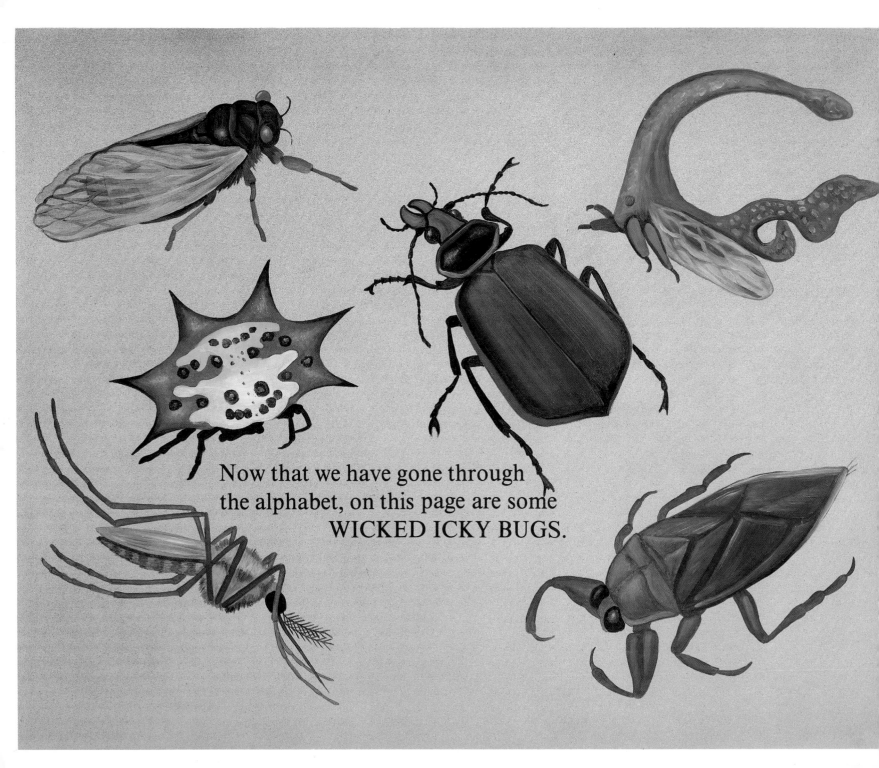

Now that we have gone through
the alphabet, on this page are some
WICKED ICKY BUGS.

Although the general public considers every creature in this book a bug, in fact, only the Yellow Plant Bug and the Cotton Stainer are true bugs. The Orb Weaver, Water Spider and Tarantula, are spiders. The Velvet Mite and the Scorpion are arachnids. The rest, including the true bugs, are insects.